Up Country

Books by Maxine Kumin

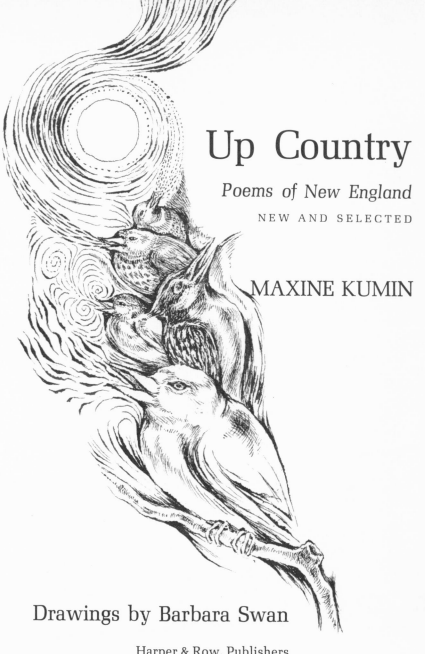

Up Country

Poems of New England

NEW AND SELECTED

MAXINE KUMIN

Drawings by Barbara Swan

Harper & Row, Publishers
New York, Evanston, San Francisco, London

The following poems appeared in *The Nightmare Factory*, Harper & Row, Publishers, Inc., 1970: "For a Shetland Pony Brood Mare Who Died in Her Barren Year," "The Presence," "Watering Trough," "The Vealers," "Hello, Hello Henry," "Cellar Hole in Joppa," "Riding in the Rain," "Night, the Paddock, Some Dreams," "Country House," "The Woodlot in Winter," "Homecoming," "We Are," "Whippoorwill."

The following poems appeared in *The Privilege*, Harper & Row, Publishers, Inc., 1965: "Morning Swim," "January 25th," "May 10th," "June 15th," "July 5th," "August 9th," "September 22nd."

"A Hundred Nights" and "The First Rain of Spring" are from *Halfway* by Maxine Kumin. Copyright © 1957, 1958, 1959, 1960, 1961 by Maxine W. Kumin. Reprinted by permission of Holt, Rinehart and Winston, Inc.

The following poems originally appeared in *The New Yorker:* "The Hermit Wakes to Bird Sounds," "The First Rain of Spring," "Watering Trough," "May 10th," and "Homecoming."

The following poems appeared originally in the May-June 1972 issue of *Audience:* "The Hermit Prays," "The Hermit Celebrates the Basswood Tree," "The Hermit Picks Berries," "The Hermit Meets the Skunk," "The Hermit Has a Visitor," "The Hermit Goes Up Attic," and "The Hermit Reviews His Simples."

"Five Small Deaths in May" is reprinted by permission of the *Berkshire Review*.

"The Dreamer, the Dream" originally appeared in *The Atlantic Monthly*.

"The Horses" originally appeared in the Fall, 1972, issue of *The Poetry Miscellany*, published in Williamstown, Mass.

"Beans" and "Turning To" originally appeared in the Spring, 1972, issue of *Antaeus*.

The following poems originally appeared in the March 21, 1972, issue of *Saturday Review:* "Stones," "Creatures," "Mud," "Cross Country by County Map."

"Woodchucks" originally appeared in the August, 1971, issue of *The Boston Review of the Arts*.

FIRST EDITION

STANDARD BOOK NUMBER: 06-012473-3

LIBRARY OF CONGRESS CATALOG CARD NUMBER: 72-79680

Contents

THREE

FOUR

Joppa Diary

One

The Hermit Wakes to Bird Sounds

He startles awake. His eyes are full of white light.
In a minute the sun will ooze into the sky.
Meanwhile, all the machines of morning start up.

The typewriter bird is at it again.
Her style is full of endearing hesitations.
The words, when they come, do so in
the staccato rush of a deceitful loveletter.

The sewing machine bird returns to the doddering elm.
Like Penelope, she rips out yesterday's stitches
only to glide up and down, front and back
reentering the same needle holes.

The bird who presides at the wellhouse primes the pump.
Two gurgles, a pause, four squeaks of the handle
and time after time a promise of water
can be heard falling back in the pipe's throat.

Far off the logging birds saw into heartwood
with rusty blades, and the grouse cranks up
his eternally unstartable Model T
and the oilcan bird comes with his liquid pock pock

to attend to the flinty clanks of the disparate parts
and as the old bleached sun slips into position
slowly the teasing inept malfunctioning
one-of-a-kind machines fall silent.

The Hermit Meets the Skunk

The hermit's dog skitters home
drunk with it once every fall,
the whites of his eyes marbled
from the spray and his tail tucked
tighter than a clamshell. He contracts
himself to a mouse under the hermit's bed.

The hermit unsticks him with a broom
and ties him outside to a tree.
He is a spotted dog, black rampant
on white. And as the hermit scrubs,
the white goes satiny with Lava soap,
the black brightens to a bootblack shine.
Next, a dose of tomato juice stains
the white like a razor cut under water
and purples the black, and after that
the whole dog bleaches mooncolored
under a drench of cornstarch.
The hermit sniffs him. Skunk
is still plain as a train announcement.

So he is to be washed again,
rinsed again, powdered again
until the spots wink out again
under the neutral white.
Inside his mouth, the hermit knows
and knows from what is visible
under the tail, Dog is equally spotted
but in the interior, grey on a pink field.
If he were to be pinned down,
his four legs held at four corners,
and slit open by the enthusiast,

the hermit knows the true nature of Dog
spotted layer by layer
would be laid bare.

Afterward all night
skunk sleepwalks the house.
Skunk is a pot of copper pennies
scorched dry on a high flame.
Skunk is a porridge of dead shrews
stewed down to gelatin.
Skunk is the bloat of chicken gut
left ten days to sweeten in the sun.
Skunk is the mother bed, the ripe taste
of carrion, the green kiss.

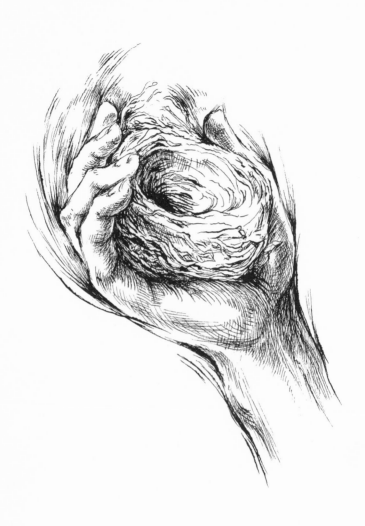

The Hermit Prays

I hold in my hand this cup
this ritual, this slice of womb
woven of birchbark strips
and the woolly part of a burst cocoon
all mortared with mud and chinked
with papers of snakeskin.

I hold in my hand this carcass
this wintered-over thing.

What they are made of, these string
sacks, these tweezered and gluey cells
can only be said of a house,
of plumb bobs and carpenters' awls.

God of the topmost branch
god of the sheltering leaf
fold your wing over.
Keep secret and keep safe.

The Hermit Picks Berries

At midday the birds doze.
So does he.

The frogs cover themselves.
So does he.

The breeze holds its breath in the poplars.
Not one leaf turns its back.
He admires the stillness.

The snake uncoils its clay self
in the sun on a rock in the pasture.
It is the hermit's pasture.
He encourages the snake.

At this hour a goodly number
of blueberries decide to ripen.
Once they were wax white.
Then came the green of small bruises.
After that, the red of bad welts.
All this time they enlarged themselves.
Now they are true blue.

The hermit whistles as he picks.
Later he will put on his shirt
and walk to town for some cream.

The Hermit Celebrates the Basswood Tree

Lady
my sweet enormity
wearing at eighty feet
a white ruff thicker
than Queen Elizabeth's
and smelling like a shopgirl
doused with rose water,
you wake me this morning
the middle of July
open to a furnace of bees
whose drudgeries hum
like the prop planes
of my childhood.

Today
you are an airfield
in New Jersey and I
am eight in short pants
come with my uncle for
a skyride over Atlantic City.
Under us the sea runs
its long tongue in and out.
The breakers freeze
into birthday-cake roses
and perfect replicas of people
have been made for me
out of matchsticks.

Lady
you cast a rich shade
that stains the early
apple green grass.
You send me down
the dime-store sweetness
of your crowded white bells.
In that way the air sang.
I buried my nose in
cotton candy and was
licked clean with a handkerchief.
Lady.

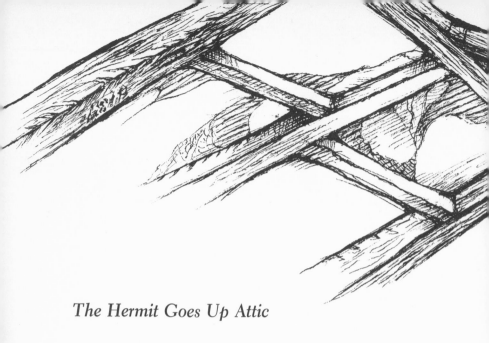

The Hermit Goes Up Attic

An Englishman went to India to make
a fortune first, in order that he
might return to England and live the
life of a poet. He should have gone
up garret at once.
—Thoreau, *Walden*

Up attic, Lucas Harrison, God rest
his frugal bones, once kept a tidy account
by knifecut of some long-gone harvest.
The pine was new. The pitch ran down to blunt
the year: 1811, the score: 10, he carved
into the center rafter to represent
his loves, beatings, losses, hours, or maybe
the butternuts that taxed his back and starved
the red squirrels higher up each scabbed tree.
1812 ran better. If it was bushels he risked,
he would have set his sons to rake them ankle deep
for wintering over, for wrinkling off their husks
while downstairs he lulled his jo to sleep.

By 1816, whatever the crop goes sour.
Three tallies cut by the knife is all
in a powder of dead flies and wood dust pale as flour.
Death, if it came then, has since grown dry and small.

But the hermit makes this up. Nothing is sure
under this rooftree keel veed in
with rafter ribs. Up here he always hears
the ghosts of Lucas Harrison's jackpines
complain, chafing against their mortised pegs,
a woman in childbirth pitching from side to side
until the wet head crowns between her legs
again, and again she will bear her man astride

and out of the brawl of sons he will drive like oxen
tight at the block and tackle, whipped to the trace,
come up these burly masts, these crossties broken
from their growing and buttoned into place.

Whatever it was is now a litter of shells.
Even at noon the attic vault is dim.
The hermit carves his own name in the sill
that someone after will take stock of him.

The Hermit Has a Visitor

Once he puts out the light
moth wings on the window screen slow
and drop away like film lapping the spool
after the home movie runs out.

He lies curled like a lima bean
still holding back its cotyledon.
Night is a honeycomb.
Night is the fur on a blue plum.

And then she sings. She raises the juice.
She is a needle, he the cloth.
She is an A string, he the rosewood.
She is the thin whine at concert pitch.

She has the eggs and he the blood
and after she is a small
red stain on the wall
he will itch.

The Hermit Reviews His Simples

If a man cannot pass water,
says the old handbook of simples,
you steep him a potion of beewort
so called because its leaf blades
will comfort the drones in the hive
and lull them back into their labors.
The hermit calls it sweet flag.
He knows how to boil the rhizomes
down into candy, a trick that
the settlers learned from the Indians.
Sweet flag—calamus—the smell of
its growing sits on the swamp air.
He walks in a clutch of dragonflies
that sew shut the mouths of bad children
and the leeches sideslip on his rubber
boots. Stooping among the rushes
he thinks, if it should befall him,
within three days he will send forth his urine.

Each year at the juice-end of summer
the hermit goes down to the river
to cheat the raccoons and the polecats
of what the old herbals call wallwort.
Bending the snappish twigs down
and careless about their magic
that laid to a snake bite will heal it
or oozed in four draughts will cure dropsy,
he strips off the elderberries.
But after his pail has grown heavy
he observes the ancient injunction
lest any evil befall him:
on leaving do not look behind you.

Cleavers—the hermit says burdock—
that poke from last winter's taproots
if peeled to their white pith, as new as
the thighs of north country virgins,
in steue will beget a man sons.
The alliums, brighter than onions
when *mixed with sallets will render them
more grateful.* To bring on the monthlies,
pennyroyal. To fasten loose teeth down,
elfdock. Take thyme for melancholy,
cucumber borage for courage.
For poverty of blood there is comfrey
and if, Heaven forfend, it befalls,
tea made from small purple avens
*will preserve the heart from the noisome
and infectious vapours of the Plague.*

But the hermit does not sicken.
He has put his June wine in the cupboard.
He has laid down the handbook of simples.
He calls the old dog from the front stoop
and goes on walking his fences.

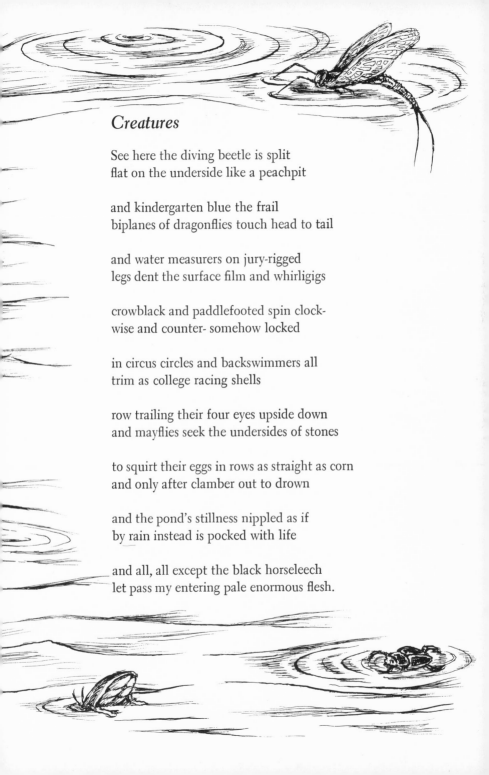

Creatures

See here the diving beetle is split
flat on the underside like a peachpit

and kindergarten blue the frail
biplanes of dragonflies touch head to tail

and water measurers on jury-rigged
legs dent the surface film and whirligigs

crowblack and paddlefooted spin clock-
wise and counter- somehow locked

in circus circles and backswimmers all
trim as college racing shells

row trailing their four eyes upside down
and mayflies seek the undersides of stones

to squirt their eggs in rows as straight as corn
and only after clamber out to drown

and the pond's stillness nippled as if
by rain instead is pocked with life

and all, all except the black horseleech
let pass my entering pale enormous flesh.

Stones

The moving of stones, that sly jockeying thrust
takes place at night underground, shoulders first.

They bud in their bunkers like hydras. They puff
up head after head and allow them to drop off

on their own making quahogs, cow flops, eggs and knee
caps. In this way one stone can infuse a colony.

Eyeless and unsurprised they behave
in the manner of stones: swallow turnips, heave graves

rise up openmouthed into walls and from time
to time imitate oysters or mushrooms.

The doors of my house are held open by stones
and to see the tame herd of them hump their backbones

as cumbrous as bears across the pasture in
an allday rain is to believe for an afternoon

of objects that waver and blur
in some dark obedient order.

The Horses

It has turned to snow in the night.
The horses have put on
their long fur stockings
and they are wearing
fur capes with high necks
out of which the device
of their ears makes four statues.
Their tails have caught flecks
of snow and hang down
loose as bedsheets.
They stand nose to nose
in the blue light that coats
the field before sunup
and rub dry their old kisses.

Cross Country by County Map

I am standing on Bible Hill, which shows
on the map as an oval of eyelashes.
To the east are those flourishing humpbacks,
Mount Misery and Mount Hunger, that
the Merrimack surveyor has put
down as Prominent Elevations.
In between lie the sleepy ponds,
Mud, Meadow, Grassy, and Long,
crosshatched on paper. They overflow,
but there is no symbol for beaver.

No one is left on these drumlins where
the roads throw up their own gates and bars
as the birches walk in, eight or ten abreast,
and the corduroy kiss-me-quicks on which
the wagon teams pulled up for a breather
leapfrog downhill year after year.

No one is left at Poverty Corners.
The map records one sugar house
as a black circle sprouting a plume,
a shingle mill, and two burying grounds
outlined in dots with slender crosses.
It does not record the headstones fallen,
the cedars gone in a blight,
the maples made into crutches.

When I fold up the map, its edges crackle,
repeating the sounds of old doors in my ears
as if down these hills the ghosts reassemble
dry as wheat, spare as stones, thin as wire,
while five miles ahead my indoor people ·
are waiting with bread and beer.

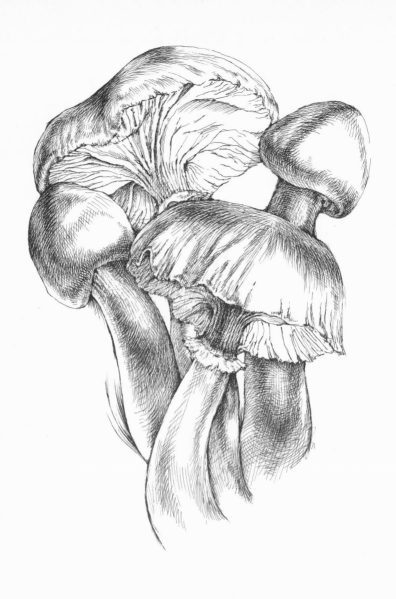

The Dreamer, the Dream

After the sleeper has burst his night pod
climbed up out of its silky holdings
the dream must stumble alone now
must mope in the hard eye of morning

in search of some phantom outcome
while on both sides of the tissue
the dreamer walks into the weather
past time in September woods in the rain

where the butternuts settle around him
louder than tears and in fact he comes
upon great clusters of honey mushrooms
breaking the heart of old oak

a hundred caps grotesquely piggyback
on one another, a caramel mountain
all powdered with their white spores
printing themselves in no notebook

and all this they do in secret
climbing behind his back
lumbering from their dark fissure
going up like a dream going on.

Beans

> . . . making the earth say beans instead of
> grass—this was my daily work.
> —Thoreau, *Walden*

Having planted
that seven-mile plot
he came to love it
more than he had wanted.
His own sweat
sweetened it.
Standing pat
on his shadow
hoeing every noon
it came to pass
in a summer long gone
that Thoreau
made the earth say beans
instead of grass.

You, my gardener
setting foot
among the weeds
that stubbornly reroot
have raised me up
into hellos
expansive as
those everbearing rows.

Even without
the keepsake strings
to hold the shoots
of growing things
I know this much:
I say beans
at your touch.

26

Mud

You would think that the little birches
would die of that brown mouth sucking
and sucking their root ends.
The rain runs yellow.
The mother pumps in, pumps in
more than she can swallow.
All of her pockmarks spill over.
The least footfall
brings up rich swill.

The streams grow sick with their tidbits.
The trout turn up their long bellies.
The slugs come alive. An army
of lips works in its own ocean.
The boulders gape to deliver themselves.
Stones will be born of that effort.

Meanwhile the mother is sucking.
Pods will startle apart,
pellets be seized with a fever
and as the dark gruel thickens,
life will stick up a finger.

Woodchucks

Gassing the woodchucks didn't turn out right.
The knockout bomb from the Feed and Grain Exchange
was featured as merciful, quick at the bone
and the case we had against them was airtight,
both exits shoehorned shut with puddingstone,
but they had a sub-sub-basement out of range.

Next morning they turned up again, no worse
for the cyanide than we for our cigarettes
and state-store Scotch, all of us up to scratch.
They brought down the marigolds as a matter of course
and then took over the vegetable patch
nipping the broccoli shoots, beheading the carrots.

The food from our mouths, I said, righteously thrilling
to the feel of the .22, the bullets' neat noses.
I, a lapsed pacifist fallen from grace
puffed with Darwinian pieties for killing,
now drew a bead on the littlest woodchuck's face.
He died down in the everbearing roses.

Ten minutes later I dropped the mother. She
flipflopped in the air and fell, her needle teeth
still hooked in a leaf of early Swiss chard.
Another baby next. O one-two-three
the murderer inside me rose up hard,
the hawkeye killer came on stage forthwith.

There's one chuck left. Old wily fellow, he keeps
me cocked and ready day after day after day.
All night I hunt his humped-up form. I dream
I sight along the barrel in my sleep.
If only they'd all consented to die unseen
gassed underground the quiet Nazi way.

Five Small Deaths in May

Somehow a mole has swum too far
downstream from the tunnel and drowned
in the pond. On his nose the star
he wears for a wise fifth hand
is losing its pink. His eyepits blacken.
Now the sun can sink
into those two particulars
and eat away the last wires.

A milk snake has come to this cup
of straw at the mouth of a rock.
It has drunk the good yolk up.
When the meadowlark flicks back
she turns and turns like a dog
making a place to lie down.
The shell specks fly out between her legs.
They are flecked lavender and brown.

A heron is fishing for minnows.
In the shadow of the bird
they crowd together
lying straight out to leeward
a see-through army in the shallows
as still as grains in a rice bowl.
Scooped up they go down whole
exchanging one wet place for another.

The owl, old monkey face
will have his nightly mouse
culled from the tribe
disgorging here and there
down in his meadow place

and at the doorsill of the house
a flake of leg, a chip of rib
a tuft of hair.

I will not sing the death of Dog
who lived a fool to please his king.
I will put him under the milkweed bloom
where in July the monarchs come
as spotted as he, as rampant, as enduring.

Turning To

Death
is what I always think of
in these connections.

We lie
ruffling mouth to mouth
making one shadow

two lukewarm frogs
content with the single wardrobe
of our skins

at home with our tongues
those lazy intelligent
lickers down

of gnat wing and fly gauze
and the pellets
of newly hatched darning needles.

We feed in spasms
at ease in a teacup
or Lake Erie

and like frogs
we are to be overturned
by any stone heaved in the puddle.

We are to be taken down straightway
by the hognosed snake
or snipped up to accommodate the heron.

Meanwhile
let us cast one shadow
in air or water

our mouths wide as saucers
our tongues at work in their tunnels
our shut eyes unimportant as freckles.

Let us turn to, until
the giant flashlight
comes down on us

and we are rammed home on the corkscrew gig
one at a time
and lugged off belly to belly.

In These Signs

If earthworms surface, if
the black snake takes to a tree
if leaves show the backs of their hands
and cows flatten like pigs in the wallow
make ready for rain.

If carrots fork going down
if the onion puts on twelve layers
if snowflakes crosshatch, falling
and the owl screams late on the mountain
expect a hard winter.

If you hold back your seeds till the oak leaf
is as fat as a mouse's ear
if you set out the eyes of potatoes
only on dark nights in March
you are in the right signs.

For the fence post will not loosen
in the wane of the moon
nor the cut hay rot in the pasture
in the wane of the moon
nor the harvest of apples show bruises.

But if the fire pops and hisses
if the child will not wean
if bread fails to rise, if the fox grapes
refuse to thicken at the boil

if there is fog in July
or the shank of the corn hangs down in September
or the wasps come into the chinking
if you should say you will leave me

I will burn down the house that Jack built.
I will cut off the tongues of day lilies.
I will walk down the white line on asphalt
from Blackwater Dam to Burnt Hill
and in the new of the moon I will
pull the eyes out of the hog's head.

Two

Whippoorwill

It is indecent of this bird
to sing at night and
leave no shadow.
I flap up out of sleep
from some uncertain place
dragging my baggage:
a torn pillow, a tee shirt
and a braided whip.

O Will, Billy, William
wherever you are and
under whatever name
this doleful bird must tell me
one hundred and forty-six times
the same story. It is
full of fear. Such shabbiness
in those three clear tones!
Pinched lips, missed chances,
runaways, loves you treated badly,
a room full of discards,
I among them.

Now the moon sits
on the windowsill, one hip
humped like an Odalisque.
In that cold light the bird
tells me and tells me.
He cannot help it, Will.
Wherever we are he sings us
backward to the old bad times.
I too am a discard
and you,
you stick in his throat.

For a Shetland Pony Brood Mare
Who Died in Her Barren Year

After bringing forth eighteen
foals in as many Mays
you might, old Trinket girl,
have let yourself be lulled
this spring into the green days
of pasture and first curl
of timothy. Instead,
your milk bag swelled again,
an obstinate machine.
Your long pale tongue
waggled in every feed box.
You slicked your ears back
to scatter other mares
from the salt lick.
You were full of winter burdocks
and false pregnancy.

By midsummer all the foals
had breached, except the ghost
you carried. In the bog
where you came down each noon
to ease your deer-thin hoofs in mud,
a jack-in-the-pulpit cocked
his overhang like a question mark.
We saw some autumn soon
that botflies would take your skin
and bloodworms settle
inside the cords and bands
that laced your belly,
your church of folded hands.

But all in good time, Trinket!
Was it something you understood?
Full of false pride
you lay down and died
in the sun,
all silken on one side,
all mud on the other one.

The Presence

Something went crabwise
across the snow this morning.
Something went hard and slow
over our hayfield.
It could have been a raccoon
lugging a knapsack,
it could have been a porcupine
carrying a tennis racket,
it could have been something
supple as a red fox
dragging the squawk and spatter ·
of a crippled woodcock.
Ten knuckles underground
those bones are seeds now
pure as baby teeth
lined up in the burrow.

I cross on snowshoes
cunningly woven from
the skin and sinews of
something else that went before.

The Vealers

They come forth with all four legs folded in
like a dime-store card table.
Their hides are watered silk.
As in blindman's buff they rise, unable
to know except by touch, and begin
to root from side to side in search of milk.

The stanchions hang empty. Straw beds the planks
that day. On that day they are left at will
to nuzzle and malinger
under the umbrella of their mothers' flanks
sucking from those four fingers
they were called forth to fill.

Immediately thereafter each is penned
narrowly and well, like a Strasbourg goose.
Milk comes on schedule in a nippled pail.
It is never enough to set them loose
from that birthday dividend
of touch. Bleating racks the jail.

Across the barn the freshened cows
answer until they forget who is there.
Morning and night, machinery
empties their udders. Grazing allows
them to refill. The hungry
calves bawl and doze sucking air.

The sponges of their muzzles pucker
and grow wet with nursing dreams.
In ten weeks' time the knacker
—the local slaughterer—will back his truck

against the ramp, and prodded to extremes
they will kick and buck

and enter
and in our time they will come forth for good
dead center
wrapped and labeled in a plastic sheet,
their perfect flesh unstreaked with blood
or muscle, and we will eat.

Hello, Hello Henry

My neighbor in the country, Henry Manley,
with a washpot warming on his woodstove,
with a heifer and two goats and yearly chickens,
has outlasted Stalin, Roosevelt and Churchill
but something's stirring in him in his dotage.

Last fall he dug a hole and moved his privy
and a year ago in April reamed his well out.
When the county sent a truck and poles and cable,
his Daddy ran the linemen off with birdshot
and swore he'd die by oil lamp, and did.

Now you tell me that all yesterday in Boston
you set your city phone at mine, and had it ringing
inside a dead apartment for three hours
room after empty room, to keep yours busy.
I hear it in my head, that ranting summons.

That must have been about the time that Henry
walked up two miles, shy as a girl come calling
to tell me he has a phone now, 264, ring two.
It rang one time last week—wrong number.
He'd be pleased if one day I would think to call him.

Hello, hello Henry? Is that you?

Cellar Hole in Joppa

o my dear skeleton

Bearing in mind the way
the earth takes back into itself each year
half an inch or so of rot,
digesting amiably enough deer
droppings, splinters of dead birds, the splay
of struck trees and what-
ever man has left behind,
we dig down in the caved-in place
we think a house stood on, its chimney fac-
ing east, still the prevailing wind.
Past pignuts and tree roots and a garden
of eyeless stones striped like turnips, the spade
clangs seven feet deep and decades
fall backward to 1805 or –10.

o my dear skeleton
what is to be preserved and why?

Bearing in mind the way
the patriarch, his wife, his livestock,
the branches of his tree—nine sons,
eight sturdy, one clubfooted, and a rock-
candy daughter—may
go down, like the chimney, all at once
in a year of drought or winterkill,
there comes from digging deep a hard
love in the boneyard.

The trash heap underneath the groundsill
gives up at last a piece of bowl.
A pot the rust has eaten down to crumbs
of blood flakes against our thumbs.
Then a blue bottle, ink crusted but whole.

o my dear skeleton
what is to be preserved and why?
is there a word to keep you by?

Bearing in mind the way
us hangers-on will also be
reclaimed, much as in the woods
where pastures were, a Model T
accepts a pine that thrusts each workday
the pole of itself more stoutly through the hood,
and seeing us rev up our automatic shift
V-8 for that one hour turnpike cruise
with quarters for tolls and Sunday supper blues,
with dog, ice chest, children, all that is left
to fall in at some undated dear
future hour, o my skeleton,
what is to be said of one
pocked blue bottle brought to light this year?

what is to be preserved and why?
Not the spoon fingers that dipped the pen.
Not the chimney maker, not the black sky
full of wind that spoke Amen.
No document of that outcry.
o my dear skeleton
no word to keep you by.

Riding in the Rain

This is the way we come
in a jingle of bits and chains
and the pocking of shoes on stone
down pasture, across bluff

old gelding, older mare
where a sweet unhurried rain
has lacquered every leaf
and the trees are chocolate bars.

The good mud underfoot
opens its matted fur
to pop up snails for pearls,
then licks itself like a cat.

Two dozen orange newts
shimmy on granite boulders
like smalltown belly dancers.
The ferns breathe cinnamon.

The horses steam out dander.
They blow their noses in
a tunnel of birch and popple.
Their droppings multiply,
a cluster of old yellow apples.

This is the way we come,
old gelding, older mare
in easy spattered air
like lazy mastodons
going from here to there.

Night, the Paddock, Some Dreams

. . . the ear has no eyelids . . .
—Ihab Hassan

All the loud night cocooned
in my farmhouse bed I hear
stones knock, an owl begin,
and the snuffles of my mare

who sleeps in fits and starts
warily upright
under the buckshot stars.
Only with the first light

she goes ungainly down
folding her leg sticks in
to lie like some overgrown
dachshund-turned-dinosaur,

her neck important as
Victorian furniture,
her backbone ridged and strong
as the Seven Hills of Rome.

She chews in her sleep, she makes
it plain she dreams of me.
In dreams and truth I rake
cut clover, timothy
wound up in vetch, such sweets
as the acreage allows.

I also dream gaunt cows
heads down in their own dung

and crueler images:
the ribs of all my dears
picked famine dry and hung
for lesser foragers.

Far worse than dreams go on.
Leave people out of this.
Let the loud night be gone
and may the old mare rouse
from dampness in her bones
and safely browse.

Country House

After a long presence of people,
after the emptying out,
the laying bare,
the walls break into conversation.
Their little hairlines ripple
and an old smile
crosses the chimney's face.

The same flies
drawn to the windowpanes
buzz endlessly from thirst.
Field mice coast down
a forgotten can of bacon fat.
Two clocks tick themselves witless.
October, clutching its blankets,
sidles from room to room
where the exhausted doors
now speak to their stops,
four scrubbed stones of common quartz.

They are gone,
those hearty moderns who came in
with their plastic cups and spoons
and restorative kits
for stripping the woodwork,
torn between making over
and making do.
At their leavetaking
the thin beds exhale.
The toilet bowl blinks,
its eye full of purple antifreeze.

As after a great drought
the earth opens its holes
to raise the water table,
the stairs undo their buttons.
The risers, each an individual,
slip out of plumb.
Seams, pores and crazings unpucker
making ready for frost.
A tongue of water
circles the cellar wall
and locks itself in.

Soon the raccoon will come
with his four wise hands
to pick the carcass
and the salt-worshiping porcupine
will chew sweat from the porch swing.
The red squirrels will decamp,
the last litter of mice go under.
Caught and fastened, this house
will lean into the January blizzard
letting its breath go sour,
its rib cage stiffen.

Watering Trough

Let the end of all bathtubs
be this putting out to pasture
of four Victorian bowlegs
anchored in grasses.

Let all longnecked browsers
come drink from the shallows
while faucets grow rusty
and porcelain yellows.

Where once our nude forebears
soaped up in this vessel
come, cows, and come, horses.
Bring burdock and thistle,

come slaver the scum of
timothy and clover
on the castiron lip that
our grandsires climbed over

and let there be always
green water for sipping
that muzzles may enter thoughtful
and rise dripping.

The Woodlot in Winter

To come among the hardwoods
in a high wind is to enter
a long-empty house of many chambers
whose doors fly open and clap shut
scraping on dry lintels. Cupboards
complain to their hinges and windows
rise and fall, teeter and fall.

Oak here breaks its heart.
Hickory drops its shagbark
and the woman-smooth beech tree
pushes nine legs through the floorboards.
Fat stones rub under the snow crust.
The rafters drink in their birds.
Only, in the inglenook the ghost
of a rabbit is having its throat cut.

Homecoming

Having come unto
the tall house of our habit
where it settles rump downward
on its stone foundations
in the manner of a homely brood mare
who throws good colts

and having entered
where sunlight is pasted on the windows
ozone rises from the mullions
dust motes pollinate the hallway
and spiders remembering a golden age
sit one in each drain

we will hang up our clothes and our vegetables
we will decorate the rafters with mushrooms
on our hearth we will burn splits of silver popple
we will stand up to our knees in their flicker
the soup kettle will clang five notes of pleasure
and love will take up quarters.

We Are

Love, we are a small pond.
In us yellow frogs take the sun.
Their legs hang down. Their thighs open
like the legs of the littlest children.
On our skin waterbugs suggest incision
but leave no marks of their strokes.
Touching is like that. And what touch evokes.

Just here the blackest berries fatten
over the pond of our being.
It is a rich month for putting up weeds.
They jut like the jaws of Hapsburg kings.
Tomorrow they will drop their blood
as the milkweed bursts its cotton
leaving dry thorns and tight seeds.

Meanwhile even knowing
that time comes down to shut the door
—headstrong, righteous, time hard at the bone
with ice and one thing more—
we teem, we overgrow. The shelf
is tropic still. Even knowing
that none of us can catch up with himself

we are making a run
for it. Love, we are making a run.

Three

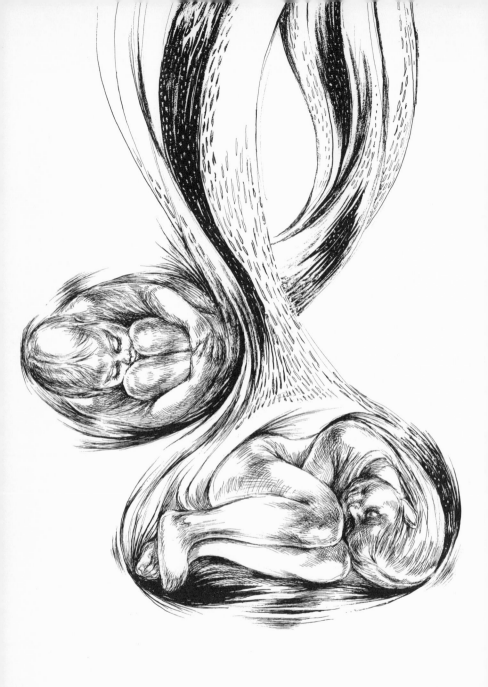

The First Rain of Spring

This is the first rain of spring;
it is changing to snow in the west.
The children sleep, closing the ring;
this is the first rain of spring.
Darkly, inside the soft nest,
the children sleep, closing the ring,
knees flexed under the breast.
It is changing to snow in the west.

We store for death's fattening
the easeful seed in its caul.
It clasps and unclasps like a spring;
we store for death's fattening.
Feel it! The fist to the wall;
it clasps and unclasps like a spring,
mindless, habitual,
the easeful seed in its caul.

Days will expand to the west;
winter is over is all.
Darkly, inside the soft nest,
days will expand to the west.
Feel it! The fist to the wall;
we hoard for life's sweetening.
Winter is over is all.
The children sleep, closing the ring.

A *Hundred Nights*

Dark came first and settled in
the pin oak rubbing on my screen.
Ten lightning bugs sealed in a milk
jar on my bureau winked and sulked.
I washed into a dream of a hunchback
chasing me with an empty mail sack

until the terrible mouse with wings
notched like bread knives came skittering
down the chimney next to my bed;
rudderless, raving, flapped and shied
against the ceiling, bedclothes, table.
I screamed as soon as I was able.

Father in a union suit
came a hundred sultry nights,
came like an avenging ghost.
He waved a carpetbeater, trussed
with scrolls of hearts and cupid wings,
a racket with rococo strings.

Two uncles one floor up ran down
a hundred nights to cheer and groan
as Father swore and chipped the plaster,
a game he never cared to master.
My father had his principles.
He smacked to stun them, not to kill.

Frozen underneath the sheets,
I heard the bats mew when he hit.
I heard them drop like squashing fruit.
I heard him test them with his foot.

I knew when he unlatched the screen
and sent them skimming by one wing.

The fall revived them, so he said.
I cried. I wished that they were dead.
I begged him stuff the chimney stack.
I pinched my lips to stay awake
to keep those flapping rats outside,
sang to myself, told riddles, prayed.

I memorized those crepey nights
with dying fireflies for lights:
the heave of wings come down horn-mad
to thump and thwack against the shade.
No matter that my parents said
it only happened twice that way

and all the rest are in my head.
Once, before my father died,
I meant to ask him why he chose
to loose those furies at my bed.

Four

JOPPA DIARY

Morning Swim

Into my empty head there come
a cotton beach, a dock wherefrom

I set out, oily and nude
through mist, in chilly solitude.

There was no line, no roof or floor
to tell the water from the air.

Night fog thick as terry cloth
closed me in its fuzzy growth.

I hung my bathrobe on two pegs.
I took the lake between my legs.

Invaded and invader, I
went overhand on that flat sky.

Fish twitched beneath me, quick and tame.
in their green zone they sang my name

and in the rhythm of the swim
I hummed a two-four-time slow hymn.

I hummed *Abide with Me*. The beat
rose in the fine thrash of my feet,

rose in the bubbles I put out
slantwise, trailing through my mouth.

My bones drank water; water fell
through all my doors. I was the well

that fed the lake that met my sea
in which I sang *Abide with Me*.

January 25th

All night in the flue like a trapped thing,
like a broken bird,
the wind knocked unanswered.
Snow fell down the chimney, making
the forked logs spit
ashes of resurrected crickets.
By 3 A.M. both stoves were dead.
A ball of steel wool
froze to the kitchen window sill,
while we lay back to back in bed,

two thin survivors. Somewhere in a small dream,
a chipmunk uncorked from his hole
and dodged along the wall.
My love, we live at such extremes
that when, in the leftover spite of the storm,
we touch and grow warm,
I can believe I saw
the ground release
that brown and orange commonplace
sign of thaw.

Now daylight the color of buttermilk
tunnels through the coated glass.
Lie still; lie close.
Watch the sun pick
splinters from the window flowers.
Now under the ice, under twelve knee-deep layers
of mud in last summer's pond
the packed hearts of peepers are beating
barely, barely repeating
themselves enough to hang on.

May 10th

I mean
the fiddleheads have forced their babies,
blind topknots first, up from the thinking rhizomes
and the shrew's children, twenty to a teaspoon,
breathe to their own astonishment
in the peephole burrow.

I mean
a new bat hangs upside down in the privy;
its eyes are stuck tight, its wrinkled pink mouth twitches
and in the pond, itself an invented puddle,
tadpoles quake from the jello
and come into being.

I mean, walk softly.
The maple's little used-up bells are dropping
and the new leaves are now unpacking,
still wearing their dime-store lacquer,
still cramped and wet from the journey.

June 15th

On this day of errors
a field mouse brings forth her young
in my desk drawer.

Come for a pencil,
I see each one,
a wet steel thimble pulled out of its case,
begin to worm its way uphill
to a pinhead teat.

As if I were an enlarged owl
made both gross and cruel,
I lean closer.

The mother rears and kills.
Her forelegs loop like paper clips
as she tears at her belly fur,
shredding it fine as onion skin,
biting the blind and voiceless nubbles off.

Later, she runs past me.
I see her mouth
is stuffed full of a dead baby.

July 5th

in the old burying ground

Stop, passengers, as you pass by
this road they voted funds to grade
and scrape for yesterday's parade—
this nowhere road, this ingrown track
to cellar holes and loggers' shacks—
as you are now, so once was I.

After the fireworks last night
climbed up and cracked the sky,
the deer came in to nip the blooms
from these geraniums

where plastic flags with fifty stars
mark such as *Nehemiah White,*
Captain of the Valley Volunteers.
He and his cannon muzzled at the wall
must lie here till Christ will call

alongside *Jane, Aetat. 87,*
who *went down like a shock of corn*
fully ripe. She stands up in Heaven
adjoining three unnamed newborns
buried on their mother's arms,
all lost in childbed fever.
Legions of angels keep them warm
for their dear Saviour

76

next to *Mrs. Susanna Gaunt*
who died in the springhouse churning butter.
Blest be the dead, their labor spent,
she departed this life in hopes of a better

across from *Pastor Israel Cole,*
a Harvard College graduate
who lived respected and died lamented
in 1778,
God rest his soul.

God rest his soul, and rest as well
Jimmy Evans, Rhoda Fell,
John Timmens (drowned) and Ellen Lee
who once took rubbings from these stones
—as I am now, so you will be—
to frame and hang, and now are gone.

Stop, passengers, as you pass by,
as you are now, so once was I
who chiseled out the prophecy:
prepare for death and follow me.

August 9th

The dewberries are in,
each one an oddball
bobbling on its own stem,
each one a unique
and bumpy cancer,
a black bulge fattening
under its leaf blanket;
some of them seven-titted,
some stunted at three,
some so lopsidedly ripe
their nibs have split.

Picking is
a disease.
To suppose we were bushmen
or redskins or a band
of lost, first-landed settlers
turned in on ourselves;
to suppose that God is watching
and does not want
His lumpish fruit to rot
is, putting it mildly,
to populate my symptoms

when in fact I am
alone in the pasture,
bending among deerflies
and the droppings of porcupines.
I am stripped to the waist.
The sun licks my back.
Brambles crosshatch it.
The universe contracts

to the brilliant interior
of a five-gallon pail.
Still making plurals,

I exhort myselves, my crew:
bend your lazy backs,
stick up your rumps,
lean on stubble and thorns
that scratch your arms;
pinch!
pull!
purple your fingers!

September 22nd

for Q. on the high seas

Reading late,
last-awake in the country,
I think I hear burned babies screaming,
screaming in the basswood by my window.
I am slow to grow used to owl talk,
slow to let it fall unquestioned
between the lines
but somewhere past midnight
can hear in the spaces
the small mayday alarms of chilled cicadas.
They are almost done.
No sleepier, I create my fear
for a diversion.

Where you are,
the long swells, secret as lava,
take the *France* and bear her
off to Le Havre.
We have our own constants.
There is a world of water between us
and the humpbacks of these
mink hills between us
and three months before we will speak
except in the mechanical click
that our portables make
talking on onionskin
across the Atlantic.

All August I leased the basswood
to a beehive as loud as an airfield.

They sucked and bottled until
the last pods scattered over Joppa.
For two weeks together
we tapped the keys of the city;
its brass doorknobs grew greasy
from our hand turns,
its pavements went hollow
under our footfalls,
everything turned dark with use.
At that time we were careful to say nothing—
we had time, that old excuse.

Now I am
in the country of the no-see-ums,
those midges finer than any netting
that blot the bedsheets all night long.
I am reminded by their little poisons
that something is going on.
Up the dirt road, two deer click in the quiet.
Porcupines chew on the willows.
A raccoon taps into my ashcan
and trails off to wash
the eyes from a sour potato.

Darling, what are your noises?
Downstairs from you, great turbines
force the ship's blind screw
to roll in its socket.
Barnacles ride unbending
on the plate of the hull.

Do you dance, play shuffleboard,
bet on the ship's pool?
Have you selected your lifeboat?
Are you on deck at landfall?
Who speaks in your dreams?

There are bat-size dusty millers at my screen.
They will overtake me if I look.
I hear the thud and bump of their longings
imitate the machinery of love.
Let me squash ten of them
and no blood will run.
Inside, they are powder,
a damp and grainy sawdust.
Inside, I am flamboyantly red,
warm, bare; as warm
as the bare bulb that lights my book.

My darling,
the leaves of the fire thorn tree
gave way in last night's rain
and a nest came to light this morning
knitted around five thorns,
its orifice so cunningly made
no predator could enter.
A pear-shaped nest,
an empty pocketbook,
an empty womb
still lined with her white breast fur.

I am tired of this history of loss!
What drum can I beat to reach you?
To be reasonable
is to put out the light.
To be reasonable is to let go.
The eye of the moon is as bland
as new butter. There is no other light
to wink at or salute.
Now let the loudest sound I send you
be the fuzzheads of ripe butternuts
dropping tonight in Joppa like
the yellow oval tears of some rare dinosaur,
dropping to build up
the late September ground.

About the Author

MAXINE KUMIN was born in Philadelphia and received her B.A. and M.A. in English from Radcliffe College. She was an instructor in English at Tufts University in Massachusetts from 1958 to 1961; a scholar at the Radcliffe Institute for Independent Study from 1961 to 1963; and a lecturer in English at Tufts from 1965 to 1968. In recent years she has taught at the Bread Loaf Writers' Conference in Vermont.

Maxine Kumin's poems and short stories have appeared in *Harper's Magazine, The New Yorker, Atlantic Monthly, Saturday Review, The Hudson Review, Audience,* and many other publications. She is the author of three novels, *Through Dooms of Love, The Passions of Uxport,* and *The Abduction. Up Country* is her fourth collection of poetry.

Mrs. Kumin lives with her husband and three children in Newton Highlands, Massachusetts.